The Harvesters

Kristen Staby Rembold

FUTURECYCLE PRESS
www.futurecycle.org

Cover painting, "The Harvesters" by Pieter Bruegel the Elder, 1565; cover and interior design by Diane Kistner; Adobe Garamond Pro text and titling

Library of Congress Control Number: 2022944642

Published by FutureCycle Press
Athens, Georgia, USA

ISBN 978-1-952593-34-5

*I dedicate this book with affection
to the people who make up the communities
to which I belong and have belonged.*

Contents

I.

II.

III.

IV.

Notes
Acknowledgments

To love objects is to love life.
The pure shaft of a single granary on the prairie,
The small pool of rain in the plank of a railway siding….

—Theodore Roethke
Straw for the Fire

I.

Some People Didn't Have the Heart to Pull Them Down

The paint had worn and the field had gone to weeds

and no one had entered them in years—
oh, perhaps the wind through a broken pane, and mice

who ran across the implements, those dough boxes and buckets,
the Hoosier cabinet that was such a wonder

with its tin sifter and storage bins
the housewife polished 'til they shone.

Out in the barn, an empty row of stalls—
somewhere, not here,

is a woman left who knows
the names of those cows,

who used to whisper them in order
to calm herself to sleep.

A Few Buildings, Gathered

Here in the afterlife, they are
stripped and stained, empty now.

They stand in a circle like a church camp,
unlocked for school groups and the last week of July.

Gone the old orchards. Gone the yew hedge.
Someone has planted a garden within the replica fence

and roses climb the arbor, so the past gives off
a sweet aroma, but does it mask

the grief and longing running just beneath the surface
when no one comes out onto the porch, flapping her apron

to shoo a yellow jacket from the jam-making,
no one skims the boiling pot,

and even the lazy and the disinclined
no longer have need of excuses?

Carpenter's Lace

The hands of someone's husband made this
ordinary palace of good intent,

the planed planks, the tongue-in-groove, the trusses and eaves
that exemplify the problem-solving of a working mind,

whatever mistakes were made,
porch aprons that rotted upward,

Norway maples that cast too much shade,
the walnut that poisoned

ground they'd planned to garden,
the poor judgments, the right or wrong of it,

whether his love was returned or wasn't,
and whoever was hurt or whoever yearned,

whether it was truly love or only effort
that fitted the windows and sided the walls.

The Stairwell

Now dove gray, now ivory,
changing as the hours pass,
registering shadows,
an eternal air of things awaited:
news and cheer to a waking convalescent,
the sight of a young husband
to a wife who has undergone labor,
a father's footfall to a daughter
who couldn't bring herself to rise from bed
because the one she loved didn't
love her back.

What Didn't Last

Fabrics they pieced into dresses, table coverings, curtains
and counterpanes, some rude and some fine,

some of a fashion, with trimmed and fitted yokes, darts,
inserts in the bodices, hand-covered buttons

made for those who were surely adored—
what became of them? Did a few quilt squares

or wedding dresses make their way down to granddaughters,
and did those younger women wonder

at the stitches running like seed pearls or at the luminescence
of those former afternoons? Did they guess

at motives that were too remote
to know—for who can know, now or ever,

of the strife, love, companionship or reverie of others?
I suppose they marveled at the tiny needle pricks.

Grandmother

Applesauce is bubbling pinpricks of sugar spit,
covering her forearms, the face of her watch,
her cheeks, even the creased, worried triangle of skin
above the bridge of her nose where the glasses pinch.

Postpartum depression, they say, is the reason
her younger daughter—her beautiful, bright,
inexplicable daughter—crashed her car into a building.
Her newborn was with her. No lasting injury.

But there will be psychiatrists again,
another dent in their savings. She is leaning over the stove
on a chill and clouded afternoon fifty Octobers ago,

wishing for her husband to come and kiss her
and taste the sweet tartness
she concentrates further with each stir.

The Farmhouse on the Brow of a Hill

If there was a mother, I never saw her.
Once, the girl asked me to play: compared
to my house, all was dusty, gray—free, but sadder.
The people there didn't labor more
than the least required, we weren't sure
whether from hardship or because they
were disinclined. We took them things,
but not enough to make them better.
All the objects were withered,
broken or unwashed, unfinished wood
weathering to silver. Every row
of every field was windward,
and the fence lines stood out like gravure,
especially in winter.

Thanatopsis

There's testimony in barn skeletons,
sagging fences that sing in the wind
coming cool off the ridge, midday
shining off silos, glare of corrugated
roofs, the telephone wires. Look forward
to dusk: guttural sound of sheep's complaint,

the baying of dogs, banged utensils,
that interval of silence just before
the low moan of cows letting down
and geese passing by on their wide circle
back to the pond.

The Way to Susan's

We glide past houses we can both name,
the faint tick of our bikes counting, uneven rhythm
of shadow and sun, past the Hunts', the Ryans',
finally, the music teacher's, the last oasis of shade
before it's all grind uphill past the vineyard,
the farmhouse with its unwashed children,
more vines. It's here she chooses to tell me
her parents have split and will live apart.
By now, we've swung off our bikes and are pushing uphill.
As I look out across the ordinary brown roofs,
the roads' gray perimeters and, far off,
the watercolor smear of lake, geography fails,
and the only distance I feel
is the sudden one between us.

Which Is More Beautiful, Autumn Woods
or the Basketweave of Corn Left Standing?

Cellulose, stalk, kernel, straw,
a hollow little pipe playing.
Pith, stem, fiber, core,
a house with its side peeling.
It's a matter for the light, revealing
the color of chalk, trunks and branches
standing out along the hillslope.
A chorus of waving hands beckons the eye
deeper and deeper into the woods.
Fluttering bright maple branches interrupt
tiers of hemlocks that weep over
the terraced stream. A wind that is
nearly visible, like crosshatching,
bends the brush and strips the leaves.

Town Line Road

She's riding close to the torn sedge at road's margin,
past wasted fields guarded by hell's dogs.
Still the same, painted rocks and tire gardens,
the curve where the barn shoulders its bulk,
the cars on blocks lying at rest, the orange
triangles of farm machinery, sumac groves
emitting their faint green air of poison, dust
on the leaf blades, a grit on the tongue.
The still air as she enters waits for her to part it,
and when she has gone, it seals closed again.
Birds on wire fences are silent, children who left
fifteen years ago still gone, farmers aging—
some died, left the porch roof sagging
without a cord of wood to rest it on.

Old Story

After two days of hard rain, the woods
look a little more tattered, and the bare
branches of older trees extending outward
suddenly appear rougher in texture, dark
like the inky branches of woodblock prints
in fairy tales that don't end well,
twigs bent like the crooked finger of a witch
beckoning you to check on cookies in the oven.
There once was a poor old woman,
but don't be frightened, don't
demonize her. It's only arthritis
troubling her hands. It can't be easy
to be her—to watch and be so wise—
and yet so unheard, so isolated.

II.

Historic Churchyard

They find the church while bicycling the byway,
down a lane in a grove of trees
with white-painted stone walls someone keeps
free of vines, someone whose remembrance
has become observance, like God's vigilance,
prayer as a kind of seeing, leveled across
churchyard and farmland to the far-off huddled
town, though so much seeing and so much feeling
can weary the mortal mind. The difficult thought
that someone could know the sorrows and anxieties
of others and hold them in their heart
makes this place holy, now as then, shaded,
untroubled, where diamonds glide and strike
through the leaves to light on each one.

Searching for an Artifact Beneath Composting Leaves

Beyond this past, further, deeper, lies
another, evident from time to time
as a glint in the soil,

corroded hook or length of chain
telling that these were not the first trees,
nor this child the first explorer
to have fled some present trouble.

Held back by latching briars
and low-hung branches, he longs
for the *away* of wagon tracks,
or an arrowhead to suggest pursuit,
a simple motive his own story lacks.

New World

That rose, so pendulant and yellow,
she glimpsed outside the kitchen window
wasn't from the slip her mother sent her with
across the ocean, where the waves moved them forward
from the golden light of her wedding day, the dappled
light of her mother's courtyard. How distant,
strange and overturned she felt
when that rose died of neglect.
Those old childhood indignities dissolved
and she felt what her mother had, how grieved
they'd be apart. So she set a new plant
to sink roots, to sprout canes, green
then darkening, splitting bark, surging,
overshadowing the arbor, but with flower.

Wife to Her Husband

I saw you as if from a distance:
you were a figure materialized
on an endless long horizon,
not yet arrived, perhaps a mirage,
but all was shimmering.
I confess I was afraid to believe
in what was only feeling.

Yet I came forward, not only
out of all I felt for you, standing solitary
at the front of the church, but also because
I wanted to become what the look in your eyes
said you beheld in me.

Faded Photograph of Rice About to Fly

Old relatives wearing summer suits
and flowery cotton dresses throng
outside the gray stone church, waiting
for the newlyweds to emerge.

The red church doors push open,
and here they come: the beloved
grandniece, the promising grandson.

The bride's grandma, the one who lives
right down the street, rips into the box of rice
she holds clasped to the side of her purse.
An ending is the seed of every beginning,

this she knows all too well,
yet she's about to fling the rice and bless them.
Her face, her squinting eyes, beam love and joy.

The Pull of Earth's Gravity

One evening in May, after a long day
spent setting in seedlings and gathering
the first herbs and greens from the garden,
a woman called her husband in early
from his discing and drew him by the hand
down crop rows and through grasses,
following the flicker of bar-winged finches
from reed to branch. They disrobed
and lay pressed close on the soft bank
beside the trickle of the creek, his weight
upon her, then hers upon him.

Junk Trees

Sweat equity, they call it. That's how
to become intimate with a person, place, or thing.

The first day we came and paced this land,
all along the borderlines, white mulberries.

They'll come back if you miss a splinter.
Little did I know how determined they can be.

A mulberry growing close to a fencepost
is a sign of neglect, neglect being all we could afford,

and we had come to know it in many forms: cracked
window glass, crumbling wood and paint,

relatives who couldn't call or come.
We had to struggle out of chaos ourselves.

♣

Here is the place I put in my shovel to dig for mulberry's taproot,
yellow as sin, long as the sapling itself,

longer perhaps than our history together, its rootlets
running for feet underground, turning off

at odd angles like the rural highways
leading to this place we've come.

One has to shovel out old cinderblock
along with rich, red, fertile clay.

By now, I've learned to admire the mulberry's
tenaciousness, to recognize and love its curious, distinctive leaves.

We knew this the moment we first saw it,
how we would come to work together, my husband and I.

The Wind Blows Where It Will

This morning, on my way to harvest the church garden,
I spot the minister standing at the door of the chapel
in her green stole, greeting someone,
and why should I be surprised to feel outside the church
and all its sacraments, having arrived in shabby clothes,
carrying my tools and my basket?
I go unnoticed except by the mockingbird
who calls to me from the cross at the top of the cupola.
At the back side of the building, I stop at the standpipe
to attach my hose and draw my water. I peer up
at leaves whispering in the verdant churchyard,
the white-spotted underside of the mockingbird's wing.
When I follow the bird further into the shaded reaches,
I happen upon the grave of my old friend.

♣

Never once since the funeral have I come back
to visit her. I put my hand to the cool stone
where lichens have begun to grow,
realizing it was fifteen years ago
the last time I saw her, the last time
my hand touched her emaciated arm and shoulder,
the sleeveless gauzy cotton sundress that she wore,
meant for humid weather, and I sat in the pew behind her.
We met when she was pregnant with her last and I with my first—
it was the luck of that overlap that gave me her friendship—
and we never knew each other as anything but wives and mothers.
At the time, it hardly seemed strange that the other side
of her grave be reserved for her husband, though
very soon afterward he remarried.

♣

Even our last phone call concerned
the latest news of the children,
their acceptances and graduations. I curled
on my sofa while she rested in her bed,

a hospital bed that stood obscenely
at the center of her living room.
Now, beyond the churchyard, out in the garden,
the unalloyed sparkling of the sun puts me to mind
of the time, driving her son and my daughter
down the interstate on a sharp, blue October day,
we were caught behind a truck loaded with hay.
Golden fragments flocked our windshield, but what we
felt was joy, not fear, though we were nearly blinded.

It is not as if she had never been.

The Sower

Since she spent her days as a mother will,
always with a child—

his fingers roots and she the soil—
she did as any woman would,

savored the pitch-dark
before the dawn or after the bedding-down,

the quiet threading of her thoughts, if the work
was ever done.

Like the sower of the parable,
she risked where the Word might land,

in good soil or among the thistles,
on the footpath or on the rocky ground.

Forsythia

I wish these about-to-be blossoms
would spark and touch the next branch
so that the flame would catch.

Their stems aren't willows,
though they rise prolific
from the marshland some call wasteland.
They rise from the same source.

Sharp, upright, and bare
as tinder—but not tinder exactly—
they scratch green beneath the skin.

I can't tell yet—
will it always be winter?

The Dinner Horn

Oh! the smell of fresh manure blows across the fields
as she looks out over the greening pasture
at the copper-colored leaves,
the bloom-fringed trees.
She leans against the raw boards
of the house from which her mother sent her
to call the men, at the end of a day
some had spent in spreading muck,
and the women hoeing down along
the garden to row's end,
all with the aim, all hastening
to be done rather than to be doing.
Only now does she pause, at the waning,
before she raises her horn to call the day.

Scissors and Thread

Scissors and thread, lying on a table, still.

Perhaps she has turned her attention elsewhere.
I remember certain acts of creation
she bent and frowned over.

Was she happy?
Please, lift your brow, stop
for one moment, stop and see me.

Seeding, growing, canning, cleaning,
cooking, sewing, quilting, children—
women there threw themselves into work, all kinds of it.

The pruners, the spade, the seed packet;
the books, the pen, the journal;
the scissors, the thread, the needle:

If you ever see them idle, you'll know I'm gone.

Troubles

Women came to tend this garden for a friend,
tore out the overgrown vines,
immersed themselves in the dust and chaff

that parched summer when almost everything,
in one guise or another,
had become wilted or tattered or tired—

their friend's illness, a son's unhappy marriage,
a father's syncope. Though they tried, no one
could make wisdom out of the suffering.

So they dragged the mat of bindweed,
the only green,
out to pasture's gate

where horses, smelling of the sun, with sweat-glazed
velvet coats, came down to greet them.

Beauty

At the hairdresser's, something made me remember.
I almost asked how was her
friend who used to work the next mirror,
the next scissors and swivel chair, who
also drove a school bus and had a husband
who adored her, often sent her flowers,
and she was a mother, and a grandmother
with two grandchildren, although
she still looked beautiful, no more
than thirty-five, and although she fretted over
her weight in the mirror—we all did.
The truth was, we all were lovely
twenty years ago when I met her,
when I first started coming, my hair
still naturally golden, my best friend
also still living near, and we shared the hairdresser,
men still stared, and children clung and cried
whenever we tried to leave.

III.

Old Boys

So far, they've never been apart,
these four stooped schoolfellows,
friends since the elementary years, who pulled
pranks and were welcomed into each other's
kitchens and are the last ones left to recall
those particular mothers in their rickrack-trimmed
aprons (certain aspects of them, their harsh
voice or soft voice or kindness), who scuffed
the floor and wore out shoes, who worked
as paper boys, rat catchers, and shovelers of coal
(their vocations never took them far),
who outgrew clothes, drank and kissed and swore,
drove as young as the age of twelve,
and learned to tell jokes with the best of them.

Sanctuary

Sometimes, snowstorms caught travelers out
on the road between this town and the next,

squalls driving flakes so multitudinous and dense,
layer succeeding layer, white into slate into white again.

At those moments, the world they knew
was caught in the act of disappearing.

But there was a house, halfway along the track
as it dipped down to the valley,

where they would be taken in,
not that they would like to ask.

After the snowmelt, all was lush—
fields, hedgerows—and that house

where they'd been the recipients of mercy
bloomed with a garden of roses.

He Couldn't Fix a Thing

Even if he'd wanted to,
he hadn't the habit or the knack
a farmer has, and one might ask
what is he doing out of his element,
standing alone in his silent shed,
drawing from his cigarette, amongst dusty cans
of screws, nails, and picture hooks,
though he hates to muse and he hates solitude?

He puts so much effort into ignoring what's broken,
he can't be troubled
to lift a hammer or any other tool
and address the doorknob that came loose,
the latch that wouldn't catch,
the torn screens and the door slamming.

Lament

It's alcohol that cinched the sadness,
though your life—did it not?—began in gladness,
and although some would call it remedy,
that belt of whiskey or cupful of brandy,
there are some who would call the belt strap
remedy, too: it bites the way one girths a tree,
it tears into the flesh with lashes,
and, if the sickness from which you seek relief
is your humor for melancholy and grief,
you would do better to starve it than drown it.
Perhaps the cure is kindness. Then one might ask,
why didn't you seek to love yourself
as you have loved many a friend?
But you sought senselessness instead.

The Potato Eaters

The clouds lower, heavy with snow, but not yet
unburdened, so the sky is a weight
that never lifts, like this body
you are trapped within, a history to be read,

a map of veins, not yours at all, handed
down like a vessel from one generation to the next.
Now it's your turn to be earthbound,
tied to your fate. Look at the dull brown

landscapes of Van Gogh, the ruff of uneven sod,
argument and rebuttal, a houseful of relatives
who share common knowledge and dread.

No one pushes up from the unvarnished
wood of the table, the carnal fruit,
the unpared cheese beside warm ale.

The Widower's Tale

This year the wisteria,
though it's the same plant
that's always grown over the porch
and more than fifty years old,
bloomed like it never has before,
with flowers heavy and purple
as bunches of grapes,
so I called my daughter Jenny
who was on her way out the door—
I just caught her—
to say I'd make coffee and put out sweets
if she came, and though she was on her way
to visit woman friends, she brought them over
and we sat out all morning under the canopy of flowers.

Green Corn Moon

That August evening, dining on the porch,
we watched as the single hill,
framed by trees, faded away,
and to the east, after dark, the moon
rose and shone like the sun
from behind the willow tree.
Insects beyond the summer hedge were raging.
We were seated so close,
my knees touched those of my companion.
I loved the other voices
gathering like moths under the lanterns,
the various inflections, timbres, colors,
wingbeats batting softly at my shoulders,
though I myself was quiet.

Fluency

So long as I'm among the living, I'll love
the ascent, the near hill and the next.
The moving point in this landscape
of farm fields and upper meadows
is myself. I love my limbs unfolding,
my legs' strength; I love to feel them, worn
and stretched. Below, the river's carved
a curve around a tongue of land.
It's loosening the pasture fence.
Hills above crenulate the slant,
ridge after ridge mounting to the summit.
I feel as yet untried, as if I could
remain as I am and keep climbing
so long as this day lasts, and this terrain.

Rooms Above a Shop

A man with his face in the cloud of his wife's hair,
thigh to her thigh, once slept in this bare-frame double bed.
Downstairs at work, he breathed in the scent of chaff,

the dusty scent of wooden drawers filled with bolts,
with screws, with loose metal filaments,
the scent from dipping his fingertips into the bins,

bags, till, the coins, the bills,
before such abundance passed. During hard years,
he let the stock dwindle, and he hid his idleness

and hid his grief and believed his wealth
was in her love and consolation, and he feared
the parting with each employee

and giving up the building, as we all face
the undoing of everything we have made.

To Hell in a Handbasket

Who knows whether he would have listened,
had he been told the country wisdom
that it's easier to mend a weak place
than to wait for a hole in the fence,
and what does it mean, good or bad,
that he was too fine to work with his hands?
Neighbors speculated on
what kind of fool or gentle soul,
for want of a twisted wire, would let his cows
wade in the river or, for want of mending stones,
let his sows tunnel under the wall,
or the fox vault, or the flock roost elsewhere—
was he a freethinker,
to abdicate the dominion of his throne?

What If

If the feed store calendar left hanging in the barn
transports you back to some bleak time
before you were born, its printing coarse and simplified,
the war recent, unforgotten—

a voice on the radio, scavenged coal and scrap metal,
your grandfather in silhouette behind the floor lamp,
abstract like shadow-play, his fingers forming a fox head
or hands a wingspan that do not bring him forth,

his downturned and often serious face already in shadow—
try as you might to cast a spell, to keep him
and the family as they were before the cancer,
before your mother married to fill her empty heart,

you can't; you can't unwish yourself to grant her happiness—
that reel ends with an empty frame and a slap, slap, slap.

IV.

Vacancy

When children leave home
in search of their lives,
however one tries to imagine them,
it's their bodies and substance one misses,
the rub and resin of them,
by which I don't mean just the touch
(the rasp of a voice is a thing I love),
not just surfaces, but whatever glows
from beneath, satin or eggshell,
the weft and warp of plaited hair
a mother could put her hand to,
and not just that, the footfalls
one expects to hear in the hall or on the steps
momentarily—before one thinks.

First Light

Rooms left vacant are forgotten
in the same blue haze
from which one was awakened,
however you reach for an impression—
any one—perhaps first light coming in
through branches and leaves,

the window between
your two beds, your sister's
faint steady breathing,
that canopied hush you knew to be
your shared being.

Absent

You can hear it
beneath the surface sounds of day,
the scuffling of a hoe or foot,
the wet flap of laundry,

persistent sawing,
a whistled melody,
the turn of a leaf or page,

deeper than ordinary silence
whenever you stop
all your bustle
and are silent:

absence
as counterweight
to the visible world.

Messenger of Morning

Before the clock-alarm comes milking-time,
awakening in darkness, half-expecting
his eyes will open on his father.

Far apart in years and miles,
he strolls the morning streets
where messengers he never sees
leave newspapers bundled to door handles,
the bread delivery rolled up to a shut façade.

Oh, to be the messenger of morning,
his father come to fetch him, his lantern and shadow,
to be the light that bobs across the farmyard,
to set the milking barn aglow!

He imagines, though he never saw it,
how a lit barn shines out to those driving past.

Late Visit

When the daughter drives up, no dogs
leap to greet her, no paws rest on the top rail
of the chain link fence, no tails fan like flags.
This, her parents' old domain, is quiet this late
September day. Paint curls off the eaves
of the house. Mother must be resting within.
Shade has deepened beneath the gnarled maple
the daughter planted as a stick fifty years ago.
Though it was supposed to be weak and brittle,
not a desired variety, it flourishes.

The only sounds besides the breezes and the rasp
of crickets are the ghost barks and bays
of Mother's Irish setters. Who can say
whether it's the house they haunt or the daughter
when she closes her eyes and once again
can see them dancing—beloved, beautiful,
and fearsome in their feathery, flaming plumage.

Rendered

A cool morning. We throw the doors open
to that late summer smell of heavy vegetation,
pond scum, a hint of underlying rot.
The rendered scent still registers as sweetness.

Go down the road of remembered sensations:
peddling a bicycle so slowly, the tire swerves;
shuffling cards in the summerhouse;
crying hot tears, thinking your heart will break;
lingering out on the lawn until a dew forms,
light softens, the dusk and then the darkness.

Today, as we walk along a side street,
I converse with a friend about her husband's
recent, worrisome, argumentative way.

New Owners

They spent all day dismantling a hemlock
that grew too close to the foundation, draped

the rooftop, rubbed the gutters.
Men swagged in soft gray ropes

handed the branches down almost tenderly
to the next set of arms like sprays of flowers

laid alongside the raw rip of the saw.
We all remember the cancer's methodical

undoing that devastated him before he died.
The house sold, and each was given

their memory or dream: one woman's dream
was his face outside her window

in swirling snow, and though she didn't join him,
he waited there until her eyes met his.

It Began with a Little Smoke

One night some years ago, sky blazed pink over snow
and the brightness woke us all.
We came running in our boots and gowns
to see the pumper truck draw water from the stream,

dousing the neighbor's family room and Christmas tree.
Now that childhood's gone and it's the eve
of my own child leaving, I had a dream
that began with a little smoke I didn't heed

next door to my parents' home, rising
from the neighbor's outbuilding
(it was mine in the dream).

By the time I woke from my funk, flame
had consumed my home, everything
down to the glowing foundation, the sloping green.

Handwork

In the last box they open
from her husband's Ohio boyhood home,
squares from a quilt lie nested, and fabrics
cut into squares about the size of old handkerchiefs—

some blank, some barely started, and some unfinished,
but a dozen finely appliqued with pieces cut by tiny scissors
they could picture his mother laboring over, embellished

with buttons, lace, embroidery, and clearly intended
for his sister, always the one thought of,
for him, a source of old grief—

one last piece of work
handed down to her by his mother.

In Vain

You knew what it was to long
when the too-brief winter afternoon
began to fade, and after so little done—
some leaves cleared from a drain, some stone
hauled from the windbreak between
        two cultivated fields,

where the soil you heard seething
beneath corn stubble and winter weeds
did and did not wish itself to come into being—
though peace was close at hand, in a vista of field,
        slope, and glowing sky.

Last Illness

Whether we have had our fill or never
had enough, whether bitterness

or gratitude is the sum of our being,
sooner or later, in a quiet room somewhere,

the countryside recedes and all that matters
is a pair of hands ministering

and a pair of hands receiving,
and the lost who have been away,

who thought they couldn't easily
be recognized or remembered,

take their places again,
and hail the command

Mensch, werde wesentlich—don't be a ghost!—
so, finally, they won't be.

Conversion

And what if I strived to emulate the bees
in closing off each amber cell?

Across the grass, the surface of threadleaf
flowers, teased by the breeze,
becomes a surface of sparkling.
Come, golden sunbeam, red-tailed

hawk flying, deep October sky.
I'll lie back, look to the crowns of trees,
the sun siphoning, the leaves transpiring,
their dizzying drawing up and up.

When does the cambium cease its layering,
the bark stop its thickening and begin its sloughing?
What if my hands and mind could learn
the faith this change requires?

First Haying

In the wake of the mower, the cut-grass smell
of plentitude and contentment floods the senses,
overcoming its victims—even those who have lost
their fathers and mothers look up from their grief
and the young awaken to the glint and surge,
broken clouds rush above the distant fields and hills,
a child's lungs fill as she soars swing's pendulum
to where she can see the curvature of horizon.
Along the tree-lined aisles of the cemetery
those family members who do the tending,
who draw up jugs of water from the standpipe,
are surprised to find themselves no longer dogged
by their sadness. There is nothing left to fear—
what they expected has come to pass.

Hay Baling

Someone like a grandfather
still drives through town on a tractor with a wagon,

the outlying fields still fill with watery spring growth
and, later, when haying takes it down,

the shorn grass will lie where it fell
along the contours of slope and valley.

These new bales are large and round
and stay out in all weather,

but what of the old square bales
pitched from the wagon, the young man who toiled

and the girl who watched for him
while the conveyor belt up to the barn

whirred and spun and turned
June afternoons into a gold floss?

Of Love

What of the hollyhocks that lolled against the barn—
were their seedheads ever dispersed,

and what of the seeds buried beneath the surface?
Can longing itself have done the work of transformation,

not upon the object, not directly,
but upon the one who longed—

that girl who came pedaling out so far,
her legs pumping, hair flying,

and stood without and wasn't seen?
For a time, all lay fallow but the weeds,

then nature sent the frost that scoured the seed
so seed husks lost all volition,

sun peeled the red barn, thaw let the fence fall in,
and flowers reappeared, but wild, and elsewhere.

The Change

In fall, when threshers would come traveling
from farm to farm, women carrying sheaves
like women on friezes,

the landscape folded over on itself,
its inner side textured like basketweave
or tweed. There's a richness.
Do you see it now?

Even the waste
is golden, prodigious,
and nearly everything, even the straw, is of use,
the imperfect, the flecked, the blemished,
the closer at hand, the more precious,

and it's no use troubling yourself over what is,
or what has been done, or what is most itself.

Notes

"New Owners" was written in memory of Pete Schwert.

"The Dinner Horn" owes a debt to Winslow Homer's 1870 painting, *The Dinner Horn* (National Gallery of Art, Washington, D.C.) as well as to Tim Wilkinson, whose 19th century family portrait taken in Souderville, Pennsylvania, helped me to visualize this scene.

In "Last Illness," *Mensch, werde wesentlich* (which literally translates as "Man, become substantial!") is taken from a poem by the German expressionist Ernst Stadler (1883-1914); actually, the loose translation ("Stop being a ghost!") is from Stephen Berg's interpretation of that poem, "The Saying."

"The Potato Eaters" is based on the painting by Vincent van Gogh.

Acknowledgments

I am grateful to the editors of the following publications in which my work originally appeared:

Antietam Review: "The Way to Susan's"
Appalachia: "Fluency"
Cider House Review: "New World"
The Hopper: "The Sower"
Hospital Drive: "First Haying"
Literary Mama: "Vacancy"
Nimrod: "The Potato Eaters" (originally titled "Winter Solstice")
South 85 Journal: "Junk Trees"
The South Dakota Review: "Town Line Road"

"The Potato Eaters" and "Thanatopsis" were previously published in *Coming into This World,* (Hot Pepper Press, 1992). "Beauty" was previously published in *Leaf and Tendril* (Finishing Line Press, 2012).

I am grateful to Diane Kistner for her sharp-eyed, insightful editing and to all the editors of FutureCycle Press for supporting the work of so many poets and for giving my poems a home. My appreciation also goes out to the following presses who have selected my work as a finalist or semi-finalist for publication: Sage Hill Press, Persea Books, Able Muse, and Perugia Press.

Many thanks to the following people for their close readings and suggestions that helped me refine this manuscript: the poets of For Crying Out Loud, who were there at the beginning, especially Susan Hull Bagby, Juliet Longley, Daniel Bieker, Joan Rough, Danny Becker, and Charlotte Matthews; the Warren Wilson MFA alumni community, in particular Marni Cobbs, Babo Kamel, and J. C. Todd; and to Joan Houlihan, Peter Covino, Renee Soto, Christine Black, Deborah Schwartz, Frances Schenkkan, Charles Douthat, and Suellen Wedmore for the rich and immersive weekend we spent conferring together at Colrain just before the pandemic struck.

About FutureCycle Press

FutureCycle Press is dedicated to publishing lasting English-language poetry in both print-on-demand and Kindle formats. Founded in 2007 by long-time independent editor/publishers and partners Diane Kistner and Robert S. King, the press was incorporated as a nonprofit in 2012. A number of our editors are distinguished poets and writers in their own right, and we have been actively involved in the small press movement going back to the early seventies.

Each year, we award the FutureCycle Poetry Book Prize and hono-rarium for the best original full-length volume of poetry we published that year. Introduced in 2013, proceeds from our Good Works projects are donated to charity. Our Selected Poems series highlights contemporary poets with a substantial body of work to their credit; with this series we strive to resurrect work that has had limited distribution and is now out of print.

We are dedicated to giving all of the authors we publish the care their work deserves, offering a catalog of the most diverse and distinguished work possible, and paying forward any earnings to fund more great books. All of our books are kept "alive" and available unless and until an author requests a title be taken out of print.

We've learned a few things about independent publishing over the years. We've also evolved a unique and resilient publishing model that allows us to focus mainly on vetting and preserving for posterity poetry collections of exceptional quality without becoming overwhelmed with bookkeeping and mailing, fundraising activities, or taxing editorial and production "bubbles." To find out more, come see us at futurecycle.org.

The FutureCycle Poetry Book Prize

All original, full-length poetry books published by FutureCycle Press in a given calendar year are considered for the annual FutureCycle Poetry Book Prize. This allows us to consider each submission on its own merits, outside of the context of a traditional contest. Too, the judges see the finished book, which will have benefitted from the beautiful book design and strong editorial gloss we are famous for.

The book ranked the best in judging is announced as the prize-winner in January of the subsequent year. There is no fixed monetary award; instead, the winning poet receives an honorarium of 20% of the total net royalties from all poetry books and chapbooks the press sold online in the year the winning book was published. The winner is also accorded the honor of being on the panel of judges for the next years competition; all judges receive copies of the contending books to keep for their personal library.

www.ingramcontent.com/pod-product-compliance
Lightning Source LLC
Chambersburg PA
CBHW070010100426

42741CB00012B/3180